dogs
horses
cats
and
other
animals
in the
national gallery
of art

by
hereward lester cooke
curator of painting

book design by
sylvan jacobson

Westover
Publishing Company
An Affiliate of Media General, Richmond, Virginia.

Cover design is a detail from
The Adoration of the Magi
Hispano-Dutch School
National Gallery of Art
Washington, D.C.
Date: probably last quarter
Fifteenth century
Samuel H. Kress Collection

Found in the prehistoric caves of Spain, the first object represented by the first artist known to art history was an animal. In the thirty thousand years that have followed, artists have continued to represent animals, sometimes because they were commissioned to do so, sometimes because animals symbolized abstract virtues and vices, and sometimes because they felt like it.

The Dog

The dog in general has fared well in the history of art. Some thirty thousand years ago, according to the records of gnawed bones, man teamed with the dog to form a lethally efficient hunting partnership. Both sides have respected their Stone Age pact ever since. The dog was particularly liked by the ancient Greeks, who named one of the brightest stars in the sky "Canis Major." The ancient Hebrews, on the other hand, were apparently not so impressed with the merits of the dog. Of the 826 references to dogs in the Bible, all are either indifferent or deprecatory.

From the start, the dog was a favorite accessory in Western art. One rule of art history seems to be that if a dog is depicted as an extra, rather than as a principal member of the cast in a picture, the artist represented his own dog rather than that of his patron. The patron may have insisted on the color of the Madonna's robe, or the amount of gold in the saints' halos, but when it came to dogs, apparently the painter was free to paint his own. Studying the works of a painter like Sebastiano Ricci, for example, it is obvious that he painted the same black and white mongrel in his pictures over a period of years, whether the scene was the Last Supper or a view of Roman ruins. This leads to a minor rule of art history; namely, if some other dog is depicted, there is reason to doubt whether the picture was painted by the master, because painters were faithful to their dogs. Cherchez le chien.

According to Ripa, who wrote the standard reference book on symbols used by painters from the sixteenth to the eighteenth century, the dog meant, above all, "faithfulness," and for this reason was the constant companion of St. Dominic and a symbol of the Dominican order, which stressed this virtue. Because the hunting dog of Ulysses was the only member of his household, including his wife, who remembered him when he came home from his travels, a secondary meaning of the dog was "long memory." Slightly less complimentary meanings attached to the dog were "adulation," "shameless love," and "botany," the last because the dog could be trained to sniff out beneficial herbs.

The Horse

Although the horse was an essential part of civilization for so many centuries, it was not until the eighteenth century that a class of artists specializing in horse painting appeared. Curiously, the horse had few symbolic meanings. A black and a white horse drawing a chariot could represent "Night and Day," and presumably because the horse was vital to civilization, it also symbolized Europe. A horse without a bridle meant "carnival spirit." Apart from these associations, the horse apparently was taken for granted—as necessary as a house to live in, and yet not ranked in the same category of affection as the dog.

The Cat

The cat has jumped from one extreme to another in

the affections of mankind and in the reflection of these feelings in art. In general it seems that when man has considered himself to be the master of all things, the cat has been shunned and feared, being the visible evidence that man could not control everything. On the other hand, when man acknowledged the power of unknown and mysterious forces, then the cat was respected and accepted as an equal.

In ancient Egypt the cat was worshiped; temples and cities were dedicated to its honor. When the family cat died, members of the household shaved off their eyebrows as a token of mourning, and the penalty for killing a cat was death. In ancient Greece, on the other hand, the cat was called "tail waver" and was not particularly liked, but was tolerated because it was a more efficient vermin catcher than its predecessor, the marten. In ancient Rome the cat symbolized "freedom," and in this role appeared on the flags and seals of several cities. During the Middle Ages, Pope Gregory the Great had a pet cat, and so did St. Patrick. During the Renaissance a pagan cult associated with the feline goddess Freya was revived, particularly in Germany, and as a result Pope Innocent VIII in 1484 decreed that devotees of Freya were witches and their cats were agents of the devil. For the next two hundred years cats and witches were hunted, tortured, and burned at the stake. In France zealots invented a "cat organ." Cats were enclosed in a barrel fitted with pedals; when people stepped on the pedals the cats inside were crushed and their howls made "music." The result of this persecution was a golden age for rats—and the plague. By the eighteenth century peace had been restored and the cat reappeared in art without its sinister tag.

During the nineteenth century, probably because it symbolized the wild untamable forces of nature, the cat once more was greatly admired. Today the cat, "man's first pet," still has a few sinister overtones revived annually at Halloween, but otherwise ranks only just below the dog in popular favor. We have yet to see a president photographed on the lawn of the White House playing with his favorite cat, but this too will probably come to pass.

The writers on symbolism in general had little favorable to say about the cat. The artist was advised to represent a cat when he wanted a symbol for "ingratitude," "rebellion," or "the darkest hour of the night." When shown together with a dog, the cat symbolized "traditional enmity." Its only good meaning, according to Renaissance writers, was "liberty"; and who would dispute this?

The Lion
Of all the animals, the lion in art has the most allegorical meanings. In general the king of beasts symbolizes "strength" and "courage," and in this role he is the constant companion of St. Jerome. In other contexts the lion means "grateful memory," "vigilance," "wisdom," "courtesy," "dignity of the Church," and when tied with chains, "reason." Curiously, in spite of the fact that the lion is a dangerous carnivore, the only uncomplimentary symbolic meaning is the rare one of "terrifying illusions."

The Donkey
The donkey played a critical part in two most important events in biblical history, the flight into Egypt and the entry into Jerusalem, and for this reason has been represented more frequently in

Christian art than any other animal. There is also a third, and less well-known role in Christian art. When Christ was born, an ox and an ass were in the stall next to the manger, and bowed their heads in reverence before the newborn Saviour. Therefore these two animals came to symbolize the whole animal kingdom which acknowledged the power of Christ.

The other meanings of the donkey stem from classical literature and are less complimentary. "Obstinacy," "stupidity," and the "effects of liquor."

The greyhound and the mastiff puppy have every reason to stare with glassy eyes at the book. According to legend both dogs were sailors who were shipwrecked on an island in the Mediterranean and made the mistake of eating honey given to them by a sorceress. This changed them into animals. The magic formula for changing them back perhaps was in the book.

"The great pleasure of a dog is that you may make a fool of yourself with him and not only will he not scold you, but he will make a fool of himself, too."
Samuel Butler (1600–1680)

"The more I see of men, the more I admire dogs."
Madame Roland (1754–1793)

Dosso Dossi
Ferrarese c. 1479–c. 1542

Circe and Her Lovers in a Landscape
(detail) Date: c. 1515
Samuel H. Kress Collection

The dog, ancient symbol of faithfulness, guards the newborn Child. With docked ears and short hair, mastiffs like this belonged to one of several breeds trained primarily to hunt formidable adversaries like the wild boar.

No book on animals is complete without the speech of George Vest, senator from Missouri, delivered in court in 1870 on behalf of a client whose dog had been killed.

"Gentlemen of the jury, a dog stands by him [his master] in prosperity and in poverty, in health and in sickness. He will sleep on the cold ground where the wintry winds blow and the snow drives fiercely, if only he may be near his master's side. He will kiss the hand that has no food to offer; he will lick the wounds and sores that came in encounter with the roughness of the world. He guards the sleep of his pauper master as if he were a prince. When all other friends desert, he remains. When riches take wing and reputation falls to pieces he is as constant in his love as the sun in its journey through the heavens. If fortune drives the master out, an outcast in the world, friendless and homeless, the faithful dog asks no higher privilege than that of accompanying him to guard against danger, to fight against his enemies, and when the last scene of all comes, and death takes the master in its embrace and his body is laid upon the cold ground, no matter if all other friends pursue their way, there by his graveside will the noble dog be found, his head between his paws, his eyes sad but open in alert watchfulness, faithful and true even to death."

Fra Angelico and Fra Filippo Lippi
Florentine, active 1417–1455; c. 1406–1469

The Adoration of the Magi (with detail)
Date: c. 1445
Samuel H. Kress Collection

**"Small curs are not regarded when they grin:
But great men tremble when the lion roars."**
Shakespeare, Henry VI
Date: (1564-1616)

The great man in this case was a nobleman of northern Italy and a power in local politics. His pet, obviously well aware of a privileged position in the household, seems to be unconcerned about his uncertain spaniel ancestry.

Giovanni Battista Moroni
Brescian c. 1520–1578

Gian Federico Madruzzo (with detail)
Date: c. 1560
Timken Collection

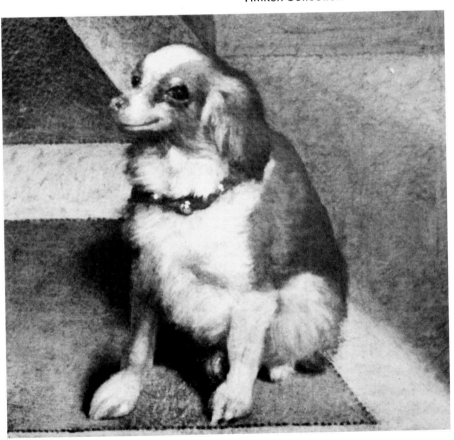

"Swift as a ray of light, graceful as a swallow and wise as Solomon." The greyhound traces his ancestry back to ancient Egypt, and has always been associated with speed and aristocracy. Here a pack of mixed hunting dogs, including greyhounds, wait at the stirrup of St. Eustace, who before his conversion to Christianity was a devotee of the chase.

"A greyhounde should be heded like a snake and necked like a drake. Footed like a Kat. Tayled like a rat."
Boke of St. Albans (1496)

Albrecht Dürer
German 1471–1528

St. Eustace (detail)
Woodprint
Date: 1501

Gift of Mr.
R. Horace Gallatine

The donkey, famed for its obstinacy, has resisted change more than most domesticated animals. The Near-Eastern donkey which carried Mary into Egypt, the Italian donkey which Carpaccio (see following page) used as a model, Cuyp's Dutch donkey used by the traveling salesman in this picture, and the American donkey of today are probably indistinguishable.

"The Ass thinks one thing, and he that rides him another."
Th. Dürfey, Quixote
Part III, Act III, Scene 2
Date: (1653-1723)

Aelbert Cuyp
Dutch 1620–1691

Horsemen and Herdsmen with Cattle (detail)
Date: c. 1660/1670
Widener Collection

The domestic cow, like most other animals brought within the circle of man's control, has changed considerably. Three hundred years ago dairy cattle were more lean, bonier, tougher, and probably were much faster on the hoof than their descendants.

**"The cow is of a bovine ilk,
One end gives moo,
The other milk."**
Ogden Nash (1902–   )

Aelbert Cuyp
Dutch 1620–1691

Herdsmen Tending Cattle (detail)
Date: c. 1650
Andrew Mellon Collection

**"To me the wonderful
charge was given,
I, even a little ass, did go
Bearing the very
weight of Heaven.
So I crept cat-foot,
sure and slow."**
Katherine Tynan Hinkson
(1861–1931),
The Ass Speaks

Vittore Carpaccio
Venetian c. 1460/65–1523/26

The Flight into Egypt
Date: c. 1500
Andrew Mellon Collection

"The lion is not so fierce as they paint him."
George Herbert (1593–1632)

Rubens was one of the first artists in northern Europe to paint lions as lions rather than as dogs with manes or oversized domestic cats. The reason for this is that he had a chance to draw African lions from life in an Antwerp circus, shortly before this painting was done in 1615.

**"Lions are kings of beasts, and yet their pow'r
Is not to rule and govern but devour."**
Samuel Butler (1600–1680),
Miscellaneous Thoughts

Peter Paul Rubens
Flemish 1577–1640

Daniel in the Lions' Den (detail)
Date: c. 1615
Ailsa Mellon Bruce Fund

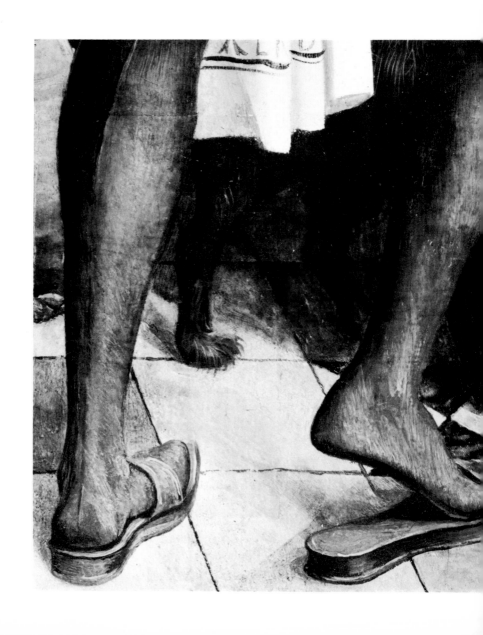

A time-honored place for a trusted dog is under the table, hoping for scraps accidentally dropped or surreptitiously slipped. The dog in this case may be an early variant of the Maltese.

"My little old dog:
A heart beat at my feet."
Edith Wharton (1862–1937),
A Lyrical Epigram

Master of the Retable of the Reyes Católicos
Spanish, late fifteenth century

The Marriage at Cana (detail)
Date: probably last years of the fifteenth century
Samuel H. Kress Collection

Manet shocked his academically trained contemporaries by painting his pictures entirely out of doors and without preliminary sketches. Thus we can be reasonably sure that Victorine Meurent, his model, was cuddling a mongrel puppy in her arm when Manet painted this famous canvas in a Parisian garden.

Èdouard Manet
French 1832–1883

Gare Saint-Lazare (detail)
Date: 1873
Gift of Horace Havemeyer in memory of his mother Louisine W. Havemeyer

The fiery Arabian stallion with flowing mane was a favorite with romantic artists of the nineteenth century and no one could paint one with more fire than Delacroix.

**"His mane is like a river flowing,
And his eyes like embers glowing
In the darkness of the Night
And his pace is swift as light."**
Bryan Waller Procter
(1787–1874),
The Blood Horse

Eugène Delacroix
French 1798–1863

The Arab Tax (detail)
Date: 1863
Purchased through the
Chester Dale Fund 1966

Most people who see Antonis Mor's portrait of a nobleman never look at the nobleman. The magnificent hound is a one-man dog, and the not quite trusting expression commands respect and care. One feels instinctively that he should be watched as carefully as he is watching you. The metal collar was developed as protection for the throat, particularly in boar hunting.

"**Near this spot**
Are deposited the remains of one
Who possessed beauty without vanity,
Strength without insolence,
Courage without ferocity,
And all the virtues of man without
his vices.
This praise, which would be
unmeaning flattery
If inscribed over human ashes,
Is but a just tribute to the memory of
Boatswain, a dog."
Byron, Epitaph for a dog buried at Newstead Abbey (1808)

"**Who loves me will love my dog also.**"
St. Bernard, In festo Sancti Michaelis sermo primus (c. 1150)

Antonis Mor
Flemish-Dutch 1519–1575

Portrait of a Gentleman (detail)
Date: 1569
Andrew Mellon Collection

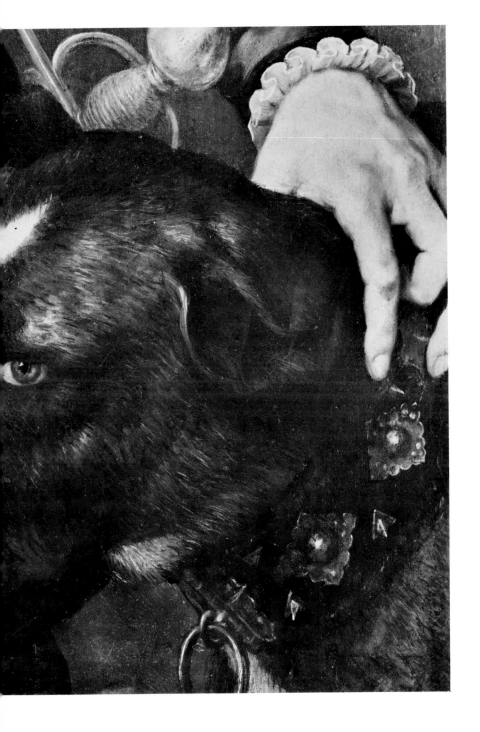

Toads cast in metal were supposedly first made in Japan, and later the idea was copied in Renaissance Italy. There is some evidence for believing that the mold was made from an actual toad. Probably such objects were kept on the desk top as paperweights.

"I had rather be a toad
And live upon the vapour of a dungeon,
Than keep a corner in the thing I love
For others' uses."
Shakespeare, As You Like It
Date: (1564-1616)

Paduan, early sixteenth century

Toad
Bronze
Samuel H. Kress Collection of Renaissance Bronzes

There were no specifications for a dragon, except that it should have some of the attributes of a snake and must look mean-tempered and dangerous. Raphael, by the alchemy of his genius, had the strange ability to change almost any object, however repulsive, into something of grace and beauty. Here it is hard to believe that any actor in the drama is really in mortal danger.

"Dear to me is my bonny white steed,
Oft has he helped me at pinch of need."
Sir Walter Scott (1771–1832),
The Lady of the Last Minstrel

Raphael
Umbrian 1483–1520

Saint George and the Dragon
Date: c. 1504/1506
Andrew Mellon Collection

Cassones, or wooden chests, meant for a bridal trousseau, were often decorated with paintings by leading artists in Renaissance Italy. The scene here represents an imaginary triumphal procession of victorious troops entering into a conquered city, accompanied by war dogs specially trained to attack horses.

"If you ride a horse, sit close and light,
If you ride a man, sit easy and tight."
Benjamin Franklin, Poor Richard's
Almanack (1734)

Biagio d'Antonio da Firenze
Florentine, active 1476–1504

The Triumph of Scipio Africanus (detail)
Date: 1495
Samuel H. Kress Collection

The reason that doves are sacred to
Venus, the goddess of love, is
because they have elaborate
courtship ceremonies, they make
love during all seasons of the year,
and they tend to be fairly
monogamous, at least for a season.

**"He did not cease,
but cooed and cooed
And somewhat pensively he wooed,
He sang of love with quiet blending
Slow to begin and never ending."**
Wordsworth (1770–1850),
O Nightingale, thou surely

François Boucher
French 1703–1770

Venus Consoling Love (detail)
Date: 1751
Gift of Chester Dale

For Thanksgiving a friend and
neighbor left a brace of American
golden-eye ducks hanging on the
door of Homer's studio at Prouts
Neck in Maine. The painter was so
struck by their beauty that he
painted them before he ate them.

Winslow Homer
American 1836–1910

Right and Left (detail)
Date: 1909
Gift of the Avalon Foundation

The prime requisites of a war horse
until firearms were well developed in
the seventeenth century were strength
to carry an armored man,
endurance to withstand long
engagements, and steady nerves.
Speed was not so important, and
probably most of the war horses of
the Italian princes of the 1500s
could neither jump nor gallop.

Botticelli
Florentine 1444/45–1510

The Adoration of the Magi (detail)
Date: c. 1470
Andrew Mellon Collection

Stubbs ranks as the first great painter of horses in the long and distinguished history of British sporting art. Regardless of rank or noble birth, the people in his pictures are always no more than attendants for thoroughbreds.

"Go anywhere in England where there are natural, wholesome, contented and really nice English people; and what do you always find? That the stables are the center of the household."
George Bernard Shaw (1856–1950), Heartbreak House

George Stubbs
British 1724–1806

Colonel Pocklington with His Sisters (detail)
Date: 1769
Gift of Mrs. Charles S. Carstairs in memory of her husband Charles Stewart Carstairs

**"The yellowest cur I ever knew
Was to the boy who loved him true."**
Unknown, The Dog

Adriaen van Ostade
Dutch 1610–1685
The Cottage Doorway (detail)
Date: 1673
Widener Collection

No one knows why a sculptor would make a bronze statuette of a dog scratching himself. This may have been a paperweight and the hound may have been a friend of long standing.

"Well washed and combed domestic pets grow dull; they miss the stimulus of fleas."
Francis Galton, Inquiries into Human Faculty (1883)

"A reasonable amount of fleas is good for a dog and keeps him from brooding over being a dog."
Edward Noyes Westcott (1847–1898), David Harum

Artist Unknown
Paduan or South German, early sixteenth century

Hound Scratching His Left Ear
Bronze
Samuel H. Kress Collection of Renaissance Bronzes

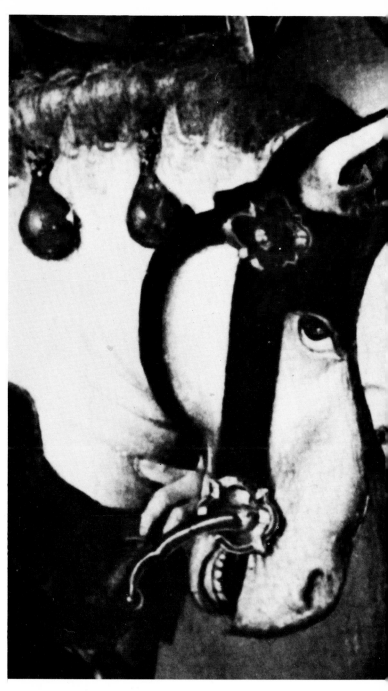

Artist Unknown
Hispano-Dutch School

The Adoration of the Magi (detail)
Date: probably last quarter of fifteenth century
Samuel H. Kress Collection

With a wry sense of humor the unknown master has painted the horse and his Spanish master looking like first cousins talking over family secrets. The tendency of Renaissance artists to represent animals with the characteristics of four-legged humans continued until about 1550.

"They say Princes learn no art truly, but the art of horsemanship. The reason is, the brave horse is no flatterer. He will throw a prince as soon as his groom."
Ben Johnson (1593-1637),
Explorata, Illiteratus Princeps

There were more first-rate painters of dogs in seventeenth-century Holland than in any other comparable period of art. The dogs were often mongrels and this probably was one aspect of the glorification of the commonplace, which runs through most Dutch art of the time.

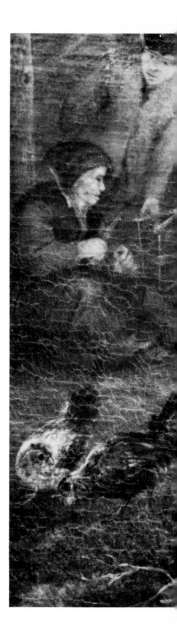

"And in that town a dog was found
As many dogs there be.
Both mongrel, puppy, whelp and hound
And curs of low degree."
Oliver Goldsmith (1728–1774),
Elegy on the Death of a Mad Dog

"If you pick up a starving dog and make him prosperous he will not bite you. That is the principal difference between a dog and a man."
Mark Twain (1835–1910),
Puddin'head Wilson's Calendar

"I like a bit of a mongrel myself, whether it's a man or a dog. They're the best for everyday."
George Bernard Shaw (1856–1950),
Misalliance

Isack van Ostade
Dutch 1621–1649

The Halt at the Inn (detail)
Date: 1645
Widener Collection

In Spanish court circles, as in most European aristocratic societies, hunting was a passion, and many breeds of animals specially trained for specific tasks were raised and kept. The greyhound's speed was used to run down and exhaust the prey, and various types of cats and weasels whose claws and teeth were lethal at close quarters in underground burrows were also used. The animal in the foreground here has defied classification, but the chain indicates a ferocious disposition.

Artist Unknown
Hispano-Dutch School

The Adoration of the Magi (detail)
Date: probably last quarter of fifteenth century
Samuel H. Kress Collection

According to the biblical account,
the Beast of the Apocalypse had
seven heads and lamb's horns. Since
lambs don't have horns, Dürer could
here give his imagination free rein,
so among his beast's heads he
represented a bloodhound, a lion,
a snake, and even a snail—each with
a pair of horns and crowns.

Albrecht Dürer
German 1471–1528

The Beast with Lamb's Horns (detail)
Woodcut
Date: 1498
Gift of W. G. Russell Allen

The pug, which probably came from China with the Dutch East India trade, was the darling of society in the eighteenth century. Goya, who according to some biographers had been a part-time bullfighter, was a brilliant painter of animals. Here with sly humor he has painted the Marquesa's pet as though the dog also was posing for his portrait.

**"I am His Highness' dog at Kew,
Pray tell me, Sir, whose dog are you?"**
Alexander Pope (1688–1744). Engraved on the collar of a dog given to His Royal Highness Frederick, Prince of Wales

**"At thieves I barked,
at lovers wagged my tail,
And thus I pleased both
Lord and Lady Frail."**
John Wilkes, Epitaph on the Lapdog of Lady Frail
Date: (1727-1797)

Francisco de Goya
Spanish 1746–1828

The Marquesa de Pontejos (detail)
Date: possibly 1786
Andrew Mellon Collection

Cats, particularly striped ones, enjoyed immense popularity in Paris during the romantic era, probably because they were safe reminders of the magnificent savage beasts so favored by romantic artists and writers.

"Puss with delight beyond expression
Surveyed the scene and took possession.
Recumbent at her ease, ere long
And lulled by her own humdrum song
She left the cares of life behind . . ."
William Cowper (1731–1800),
The Retired Cat

Auguste Renoir
French 1841–1919

Woman with a Cat (detail)
Date: c. 1875
Gift of Mr. and Mrs. Benjamin E. Levy

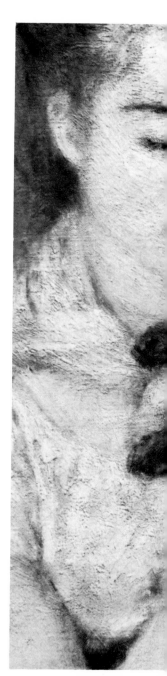

More than any other animal, the lamb is associated with Christ and with the words of St. John the Baptist, "Behold the Lamb of God."

**"Gave thee clothing of delight,
Softest clothing, wooly, bright,
Gave thee such a tender voice
Making all the vales rejoice?
Little Lamb who made thee?
Dost thou know who made thee?"**
William Blake, The Lamb (1798)

El Greco
Spanish 1541–1614

The Virgin with Saint Inés and Saint Tecla (detail)
Date: 1597–1599
Widener Collection

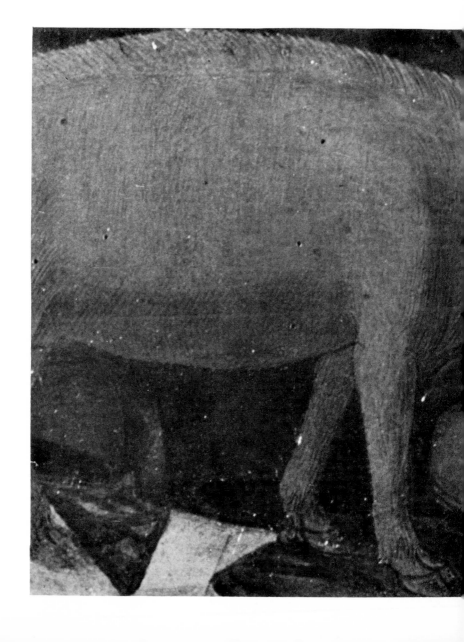

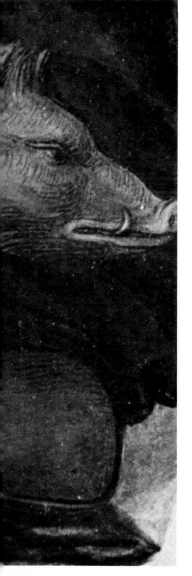

Pigs have had bad press in the history of art, chiefly because of the legend of St. Anthony Abbot. According to the medieval account St. Anthony, after a grueling war of nerves with the devil, emerged victorious and his adversary was changed into a pig, which followed around at the Saint's heels. Painters almost always showed the pig with a disgruntled expression like the one above.

"An ass is beautiful to an ass, and a pig to a pig."
John Ray (1628–1705),
English Proverbs

Neroccio de' Landi
Sienese 1447–1500

Madonna and Child with Saint Anthony Abbot and Saint Sigismund (detail)
Date: c. 1495
Samuel H. Kress Collection

"Pigs is Pigs."
Ellis Parner Butler,
Title of a story (1906)

A hobgoblin, half human, half reptile, holds aloft what looks like a mortgage note, purloined out of the dying miser's money coffer. This illustrates a popular manual called Ars Moriendi and was a reminder of the folly of saving money on earth.

"From ghoulies and ghosties and long-leggity beasties and things that go bump in the night, Good Lord, deliver us!"
Anon. Scottish Prayer

Hieronymus Bosch
Flemish c. 1450–1516

Death and the Miser (detail)
Date: probably c. 1490
Samuel H. Kress Collection